Her Serene Highness
PRINCESS GRACE OF MONACO

TREVOR HALL

Designed by Philip Clucas MSIAD

Produced by Ted Smart and David Gibbon

GREENWICH HOUSE

Princess Grace with Frank Sinatra in Los Angeles 1980.

Top: *The unsuspecting wife in Hitchcock's thriller 'Dial M for Murder'.* **Above:** *Fencing practice during a lull in the making of 'The Swan', directed by Charles Vidor and co-starring Charles Jourdan and Alec Guinness.* **Right:** *A portrait of elegance and beauty that typified the Kelly image.*

"For many of us, this suffering has become an outrage." So said the Archbishop of Monaco in his simple, heartfelt funeral oration over the body of his country's most beloved figure. What grieving citizen, friend, admirer or relative did not find justice in those words, so calmly spoken amid the frenzy of public and private mourning. Here, at the Cathedral of St Nicholas, in the heart of what is normally the happiest of principalities, lay Monaco's icon, a woman to whom the dignity of Serene Highness was never more aptly granted, and whose sudden and cruel death

Below: A 'still' from 'The Country Girl'. Her role was to win Grace Kelly the coveted 'Oscar' for best actress. **Right:** *Portrait of a princess, taken in 1956, the year of her fairytale marriage.*

Above: *'High Noon' with Garry Cooper, made in 1951.* **Right:** *Princess Grace with Ingrid Bergman backstage in London's Cambridge Theatre in 1971.*

Above: *With John Ericson near Griffith Observatory, overlooking Los Angeles, during a film break.* **Top right:** *At a Hollywood function with Maurice Chevalier. Wedding plans were already well under way.* **Right:** *A prophetic backdrop. The breathtaking Biltmore estate, built by George Vanderbilt in 1895, was Grace Kelly's screen home for the film 'The Swan'. Seen here with co-star Charles Jourdan.*

took her from the bosom of her stricken family and from the midst of an anguished people.

Above her gleaming black ebony casket, surmounted by a heavy Crucifix and covered by the fresh white flag bearing the Prince of Monaco's Arms, four massive black drapes sweeping

Above: *On the set of Hitchcock's 'To Catch a Thief'.*
Top right: *In conversation with a youthful Alec Guinness at a Hollywood party.*
Right: *Congratulations from Bob Hope following the announcement of Grace Kelly's Academy Award success.*

down from the roof proclaimed both grandeur and grief. All round, tall lighted candles soared from candle-holders decked with crisp, pink roses in prime bloom, which echoed her enchantment with the simple, unsurpassable beauty of flowers. Alongside stood her husband and elder children; Prince Rainier, in agonies of distraction, absent-mindedly crumpled his black-lined service sheet between his black leather gloves; Princess Caroline, thankfully reconciled with her mother after the distressing episode of her marriage and divorce, sobbed freely and unashamedly; Prince Albert, the heir in whose favour his father's abdication is now even more widely expected, strove manfully to restrain all public display

of his innermost emotions. All of them, by a cruel stroke of protocol, were positioned just out of physical reach of one another, unable to comfort by touch, unwilling to turn the head to catch the eye in these intensely personal and intimate moments, and each a soul of loneliness and despair, united only in the bitterness of their sorrowing and their numbing sense of incalculable loss. In

Stills from two of Grace Kelly's best known films: 'To Catch a Thief' **below,** *and 'Rear Window'* **right.**

the body of the Cathedral a congregation of royalties, diplomats, politicians, officials, the cream of Hollwood's past and present celebrities and a host of personal friends gave hushed, unobtrusive support, all standing like statues, moving only to cross themselves and to fan away the intruding heat.

Encompassing them all wafted the heavy perfume of incense

Right: *With James Stewart in 'Rear Window'.* **Below:** *The intended victim of the 'perfect crime' in 'Dial M for Murder'.* **Bottom left:** *On the set of 'Rear Window' with Alfred Hitchcock, and* **right** *with the wheelchair-bound James Stewart in a scene from the same film.*

13

On 19th April 1956, Grace Kelly, Irish-American film star from Philadelphia, married the dashing Prince Rainier, head of the Grimaldi family, the oldest established ruling house in Europe.

Monaco Cathedral provided the setting for the religious ceremony in this storybook wedding that captured the hearts and imaginations of people throughout the world. The civil ceremony had taken place the day before, in the Palatine chapel of the Grimaldi Palace.

Right: *Princess Grace swimming with baby Stephanie and her eldest child Princess Caroline.* **Bottom:** *Princess Grace in baseball attire during America Week in Monaco.* **Below:** *The family on holiday in Gstaad.* **Bottom centre and bottom right:** *Looking every inch a princess at a ball in Monaco.*

Below: *Her legendary beauty and universal popularity made Princess Grace the centre of attention wherever she appeared.* **Bottom:** *With Mr. Ormondy.* **Right:** *With Alfred Hitchcock, who was quick to notice her screen potential and starred her in a number of his films.*

Right and far right: *Princess Grace at the Palm Beach in Cannes in 1970; one of a number of distinguished guests at a Côte d'Azure Yacht Club function.*

and the ceremonial and ecclesiastical sounds of death in the purple. Muffled drums had set a sinister tempo to the slow march into the Cathedral precincts. Bugles signalled points of arrival and departure. Somewhere aloft, three melodic bells rang a sweet but tuneless toll, until they ceded prominence to the mournful monotone of a single chime. The little choir, huddled behind the High Altar, chorused its sweet-voiced, medieval chants. Its most eminent treble performed his solo part in Faure's *Pie Iesu*, earnest and positive against the background of murmuring prelates. Psalm 129— "From the depth of my misery I cry unto thee

Top: *Princess Grace sightseeing in Persepolis.* **Above:** *Ever fond of children, Princess Grace engages a youngster in conversation during a school visit at Christmas.* **Pictures right:** *The evergreen princess at various functions.*

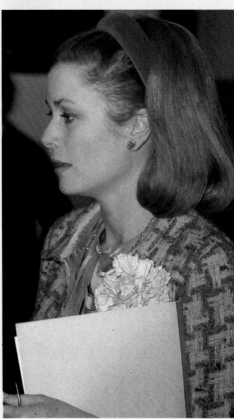

Right, and below: *The princely family pictured together during their annual winter break at Gstaad.* **Bottom left:** *Skiing was a recreation of which the Princess was particularly fond.* **Bottom right:** *Princess Grace with her children; Caroline, Albert and Stephanie.*

Fund-raising is an activity that one frequently associates with royalty, and Princess Grace's presence was endlessly requested at such functions. **Bottom and bottom far right:** *The Princess arrives at the Rothschild dinner, an event organised to raise money for building restorations at Versailles.*

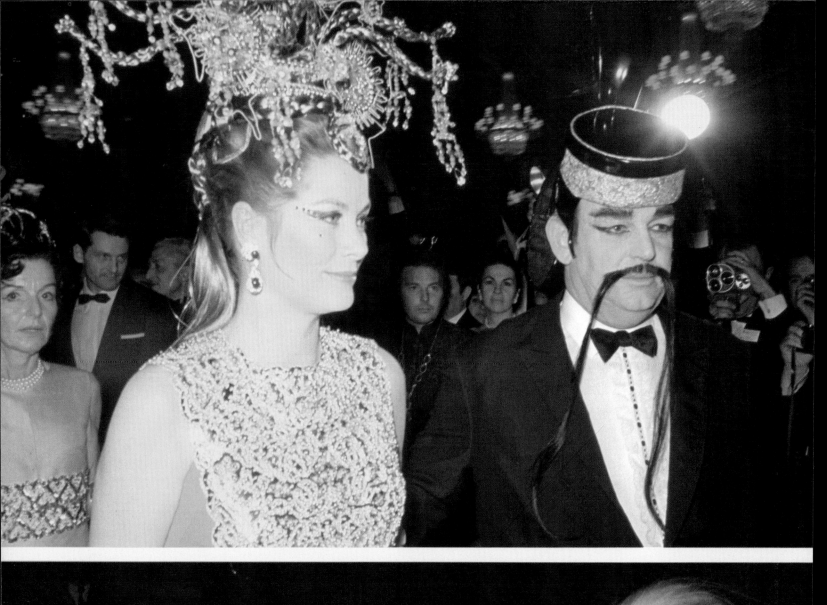

O Lord," — expressed the torture in hearts and minds.
The soaring, searing strains of Barber's *Adagio for Strings*—her
favourite piece of music— accompanied the final, emotional wrench,
soothed only by the misty chorale *In Paradisum*.

Pictures top right and far right:
*As honorary President of
the World Association
of the Friends of Children
(A.M.A.D.E.), Her Serene
Highness attended many
fund-raising functions.*

*Princess Grace, escorted by a
heavily disguised Prince
Rainier, **opposite page top**,
attends a Monaco fancy-dress
ball. **Opposite page bottom:**
The royal couple at a ball held
at the famous Monte Carlo
Casino, the theme of the event
being 'la belle epoque'.*

And the flowers were everywhere, as if designed to compensate
for the loss of future years. Each mourner in the crowded procession
through the narrow, winding streets from the Grimaldi Palace
to the Cathedral carried a huge bouquet of them—pink, white,
purple, soft mauve. More were banked so high and thick against
the walls of the Cathedral as to give it the appearance of a well-
established and beautifully-tended garden. There, as within,

*The Princess' legendary beauty and love of flowers are perfectly captured in the photograph shown **left**.*

Below: *The Princess, elegant as always, attends the Monaco national feast celebrations.*
Right and bottom: *A natural smile and her generally happy nature endeared the Princess to all who met her.* **Bottom far right:** *The Princess' interest in rowing stems from her brother's former involvement in the sport. Here she watches a race between the Oxford and Cambridge crews in Paris.*

Below and right: *Princess Grace escorts her youngest daughter, Stephanie, to school at the beginning of a new term.*

Above: *A rare moment of relaxation in a diary full of official engagements; the Princess at Palm Beach, Monaco.*

It is easy to forget that even a figure as public as a princess has a private life that the camera sees on only rare occasions **right. Bottom right:** The annual Grand Prix focuses the eyes of the world on this diminutive nation.

Princess Grace's immaculate dress sense and classic features were what the world had come to expect of true royalty.

deep, pastel pink was dominant, combining the traditional rich colour of beauty and the tempering shade of sorrow and respect. Relief was afforded only by the occasional dash of white gladioli and lilies, and the sombre green spray of family flowers resting upon the casket. Was ever tribute better paid to one whose life was never complete without flowers? They had come from all parts of the small principality, and from sympathisers as notable and distinguished as the American President, and as modest as the Princess Grace Hospital in London's West End, which specialises in the treatment of handicapped children, and with whom Princess Grace herself kept in regular contact.

Where the form of service allowed, the prayers reflected the universal agony—"the manner of her death has only added to our grief"—while the final gestures and ceremonies—the swinging

Top: *Princess Grace attends a Josephine Baker spectacular.* **Above and top right:** *A mourning Princess at the funeral of the noted black singer Josephine Baker.* **Right:** *Despite her premature retirement from show-business, Princess Grace continued to take an active interest in the performing arts.*

of thurible and asperger over the casket, the blessing of the sacred remains and the brief but significant touching of the casket as the perfumed incense drifted up to symbolise the redemption of the soul—completed the solemn, cathartic tribute and released mourners to the bright sunshine outside, where a mass of ordinary, incredulous onlookers waited to see their broken-hearted sovereign.

That feeling of disbelief was encouraged by the unusualness of universal, spontaneous and helpless grief at the height of a summer season. The brilliance of Monte Carlo's sunshine seemed

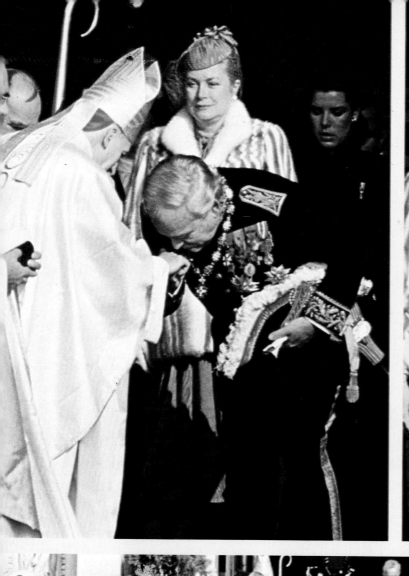

irreconcilable with events, and hopelessly out of place as a backdrop to the intense ache of mourning. It was as sacreligious to credit that the superlative season of this most sparkling of millionaires' playgrounds could be so instantaneously suspended, as it was to believe anything so fundamental and horrific as the brutal death of

its most admired citizen and idol.

Even the Monegasques, who had been close to the tragedy from the start, could not accustom themselves to the strange shuffle of feet, the hushed whisper of voices, in the town they knew and loved as the centre of the high life. Their tributes had begun three days before when, shortly after four o'clock on the afternoon of 15th September, the aweful *dénouement* came to pass. In the Palatine Chapel of the Grimaldi Palace—the scene of her civil marriage to Prince Rainier twenty-six years previously, and of the christening of each of her three children—Princess Grace,

Below: Princess Grace attends a ball in aid of the International Red Cross organisation in Monaco 1977, accompanied by Cary Grant with whom she had worked during her brief film career.

hands clasped round the flowing rosary, lay at peace, reposed in a casket whose pure, stark ebony contrasted with the rich lining and furnishings of finest satin.

The merest shadow of a smile perpetuated the elegant, unbreachable legend. Even with her natural colour strangely drained from those features set in the pool of pale light cast by a

Right: *Princess Caroline with her fiance Phillipe Junot at the Royal Palace in Monaco in 1977.* **Remaining pictures:** *The entire population of the small Principality shared in the happiness of Princess Caroline's wedding day.*

single overhead beam, she was the familiar Grace; Princess of Monaco, princess of Hollywood, princess of hearts the world over. Princess of Heaven too? So thought her old mentor, Sister Frances Joseph: "The world has lost an example of lovely motherhood, but Heaven has gained an intermediary. She's going to be telling God about us." The idea seemed not impossible, as she lay lightly dressed in white lace, surrounded by the flowers she loved, her regal, serene face defying in death all trace of the last, agonising tortures of life. Bells tolled almost dreamily from the crenellated towers of the famous pink and grey palace; two hundred feet below

the waters of the Mediterranean crashed against the vast rocks on which it stands.

The mournful, yet alluring privilege of witnessing the three-day lying-in-State was reserved to only a seventh of Monaco's population of 35,000—those indigenous citizens whose forebears have since time immemorial owed and paid allegiance to thirty generations of Grimaldis. At their head Prince Rainier himself pre-empted the first few minutes: head bowed, disbelieving and devastated by grief, accompanied by his motherless children

Albert and Caroline. With them, briefly, was Robertino Rosselini, Caroline's most recent escort, and son of her mother's recently dead friend, Ingrid Bergman. Finally the doors opened to a long, weeping line of citizenry, many formally dressed and sweltering in the impossibly hot weather, while the Prince's standard flew at half mast and the red and white flags lining the streets of the old town carried their black ribbons and bows. Within the hushed, echoing chapel, desultory sobbing broke the silence, and nuns prayed reverently, sibilantly, from the foot of the open casket. For a short while, Prince Rainier watched as the world mourned with him and his principality.

For there could never have been any doubt of the world's shock and grief over the tragedy—dynastic, national and personal—which had befallen this nation-state of less than five hundred acres. The Monegasque radio and television announcements of their Princess' death were tinged with that same sense of horror—"May God have mercy," said one newsreader—but the immediate tributes from other nations were equally shot through with outrage and bewilderment. Mrs. Nancy Reagan kept repeating, "I can't

Below: *The Prince and Princess present the winner's trophy to Jody Scheckter, victor in the 1977 Monaco Grand Prix.* **Centre and bottom left:** *A cold but happy group on their winter holidays.* **Bottom right:** *With school children in Lisbon during an official visit.* **Facing page:** *Informal moments in the life of a Princess.*

Below and bottom: Princess Caroline and Phillipe Junot attracted the attention of the world's Press both before and after their marriage.

believe it, I can't believe it!'' Queen Elizabeth's message, unusually, remained unpublished because of its intensely personal nature. Bob Hope said simply, but profoundly, ''The world loses a great lady, and I lose a personal friend.'' In a significant reversal of protocol, King Baudouin of the Belgians appointed his brother to attend the funeral, but travelled personally to Monte Carlo with Queen Fabiola to comfort Prince Rainier as soon as he heard the news. How ironic that the King's own mother, the beautiful, popular, Swedish-born Queen Astrid—a legend in her life-time as Princess Grace was in hers—should herself have been killed in a car accident on a mountain road in Switzerland in 1935, an event which plunged the Belgians into the same inconsolable sorrow in which Monaco now found itself.

To believers and atheists alike the quirks of Providence never cease to amaze, and sometimes stupefy. Certainly the tragedy which befell Princess Grace, and the controversy which surrounded it established the most indecorous and inappropriate circumstances in which someone as sophisticated, almost fragile, as she should have to depart this life. If in one way it was symbolic of the whirling life of Monaco's wealthy, influential families—for she was at the time returning from the Rainiers' luxurious weekend retreat to their glittering palace—it was in many other ways an obscenity.

Top left and bottom: *Stephanie, youngest daughter of the Prince and Princess of Monaco.*
Above: *A happy family group at their winter home in Gstaad.*
Top right: *An accomplished artist, the Princess poses beside one of her collages of pressed flowers at the Drouant gallery in Paris.* **Centre right:** *Prince Rainier is an enthusiastic tennis player and the sight of the family at the courts in Monte Carlo was a common one.*

Below and bottom left: *The Princess lecturing at Pennsylvania university, one of the many duties of which the public may be unaware.*
Right: *The Prince and Princess with their daughter Caroline and her husband Phillipe Junot.* **Bottom right:** *The Princess in Paris in 1981, presiding over a gala evening for the benefit of the American Centre, at which Gene Kelly gave a virtuoso performance.*

The sheer horror of the accident, the unexplained collapse of the official assurances that her life was out of danger, the squabbles over the legal implications, the suspicions and accusations of concealment—this was no way for such a Princess to take her leave of the world.

And appropriately, those who knew her, loved her, followed her

These pages: *A much loved Princess caught in expansive, thoughtful and attentive moods.*

Right: The Princess, as always the centre of attention, is here seen dining with Phillipe Junot, Princess Caroline's husband. Below: With Madame Pompidou, widow of the French President, and far right with Madame Valery Giscard d'Estaing.

fortunes and shared her few troubles will remember her differently. Her adoptive countrymen will worship her memory as one who brought happiness to their reigning Prince and dignity and purpose to their national interests and everyday life. Every American will

Right: The Princess with brother Jack. Prince Albert and Princess Caroline far right and with their parents below. Facing page top: The Rainiers attend the 1981 women's Wimbledon tennis finals accompanied by Lady Diana Spencer and members of the British Royal family. Facing page bottom: Princess Grace in Japan. The royal couple, with daughter Stephanie, visited Japan in 1981, and were received by Emperor Hirohito.

love her, for there is nothing that great republic loves better than royalty and she, as Frank Sinatra said, "was a princess from the moment she was born." Every Irishman will claim her as his own; indeed on the day of her funeral they talked of making her ancestral home in county Mayo into a national memorial to her. She will be universally remembered for her perpetuation of things beautiful. For those sublime rose and poetry readings she gave frequently and regularly in aid of good causes the world over. How tragic that she died only a fortnight before she was due to take part in a

"Mosaic of Words and Music" at St George's Chapel, Windsor Castle. For her association with flowers, too: her beautifully-produced book on flower-arranging, the popular flower festival *Floralia* which she instituted, the Garden Club she founded. She had loved flowers since childhood; she even stole them from neighbouring gardens to sell at her mother's charity stalls, and

Below: *Princess Grace dances with her son, Prince Albert.* **Bottom:** *At the wedding of her brother Jack Kelly in Philadephia.* **Right, bottom right:** *The royal couple celebrated their silver wedding anniversary in the United States.* **Facing page:** *Princess Grace with Barbara Sinatra.*

she received them, many and often, from admiring escorts to local hops. For her artistry with petit-point embroidery, and for the pride she felt when at last she completed a complicated embroidered waistcoat for Prince Rainier: she once said it was taking her so long that she would finish it in Heaven. For her good works in Monaco —a legacy from the crusading days of her caring mother; the Princess was President of the Red Cross, Patron of Guides and Scout Movements, with whom she used to tramp for miles, benefactor of the World Association of Friends of Children.

Bottom left: *Princess Grace at the 1982 Red Cross Gala Ball in Monaco.* **Right:** *Presenting prizes at the Circus Festival.* **Bottom right:** *With Frank Sinatra and Gregory Peck, at a function in Los Angeles at which the singer received the Variety Club Humanitarian of the Year award.*

But how adequately to express and do justice, in cold print, to those qualities which will mark her out as Monaco's twentieth-century heroine? No words could properly project the cool elegance which had made her a natural for the film screen, the groomed, magazine image hiding the sensuality which attracted suitors with marriage in mind, and film directors with an eye on the box office —"Ice on the surface, and fire down below," Hitchcock called it in his usual, unflattering, down-to-earth way. Who could recreate that

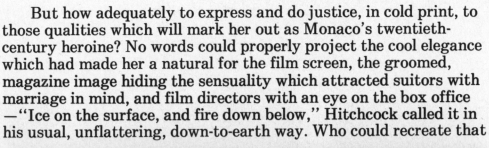

lasting self-assurance which prompted her to refuse outright those second-rate film-scripts, and later to walk with kings, nor lose the common touch? That same firmness of mind made it easy for her to turn her back on a Hollywood career that would have brought her phenomenal success, and she explained her feelings in the same

Princess Stephanie shares her family's enthusiasm for winter sports. **Top:** *Watching them skiing at Gstaad.* **Remaining pictures:** *17th birthday portraits; alone and with her father.* **Facing page:** *Princess Grace shortly after her 51st birthday*

straighforward manner: "When I was acting I wasn't a very happy person. It was not much fun to have success and no-one to share it with. I didn't regret for a second giving up acting."

Though only her closest friends knew or saw it, she had an earthy, almost mischievously bubbling humour: what other princess would be seen quaffing lager from a can, while wearing a tiara, backstage during the Night of a Thousand Stars in New York? But the poised coiffed image must prevail—she was stylish without wanton extravagance, enticing without being meretricious,

Facing page, top and right:
Joint guests of honour; Princess
Grace, Prince Charles and
Lady Diana on her official
debut. They met at a reception
prior to attending a music
recital at the Goldsmiths Hall,
London. **Above:** *Princesses*
Stephanie and Caroline
pictured together, and with
their parents **top right.**

"that sort of beauty," as Prince Rainier himself said, "which grows
on you." Those soft, confident, aristocratic features, now gone for
ever, seemed to be changeless, as the inevitable succession of Press
articles—*Princess Grace at 30, Princess Grace at 40, Princess
Grace at 50*—clamoured to point out to readers who never tired of
being told.

Age did not weary her, nor the years condemn. She never lost
that freshness, regal beauty and—yes, grace is the word—which
had pleased her Prince at Cannes in 1955 and prompted him to ask
her to be his wife. And Monaco took its cue from him. At their

A tragedy that transcended national borders, brought the life of a universally admired princess to an untimely end. The funeral took place on 18th September 1982 and drew shocked mourners to Monaco from all parts of the world.

exquisitely romantic wedding the next year, fifteen thousand journalists and a television network supplied by the new Eurovision system, recorded every minute of the ceremonies. A thousand doves were released as they ended, and the marina at Monte Carlo was

strewn with roses and lilies, and with the red and white carnations which Aristotle Onassis dropped from his private yellow aircraft. As the couple — the new princess in a dress of purest white, glittering with twelve hundred pearls, and the proud, happy prince

Despite the tributes, nothing could console the mourning royal family, whose grief was more than evident at the state funeral.

festooned in medals and the massive Stars of six dynastic Orders— waved in exultation from the palace balcony, ships in the harbour signalled "Good Luck, Gracie!"

On Tuesday, 14th September 1982, her good luck ran out for ever. With it disappeared the happiness of an entire sovereign state. Prince Rainier and his bustling, thriving principality grieve together as widowers.

The 1982 edition is published by Greenwich House, a division of Arlington
House, Inc., distributed by Crown Publishers, Inc.
h g f e d c b a
Colour separations by REPROCOLOR LLOVET, S.A., Barcelona, Spain.
Display and text filmsetting by FOTOCOMPOSICIÓN LLOVET, S.A., Barcelona, Spain.
Printed and bound in Barcelona, Spain by RIEUSSET and EUROBINDER.
©1982 Text: COLOUR LIBRARY INTERNATIONAL LTD.,
   99, Park Avenue, New York, N.Y. 10016, U.S.A.
© 1982 Illustrations: KEYSTONE PRESS AGENCY, London and GAMMA, Paris.
ISBN 0-517-402823

Featuring the photography of FRANCIS ABESTEGUY,
MICHEL, GUIFRAY, BERTRAND LAFORET, GIRIBALDI, et

D.L.B.: 31225-82